Cavalier King Charles Spaniel For Amateur

The Complete Cavalier King Charles Spaniel Dog Beginners Guide, Facts ,Caring ,Health ,Exercises And Training Your Own Cavalier King Charles Spaniel

Roy Moyes

TABLE OF CONTENTS

INTRODUCTION

The King Charles Cavalier is well disposed towards different pets, canines, and outsiders. At the point when it is outside, its actual spaniel nature assumes responsibility and it is enamored with investigating, pursuing, and sniffing. This lively, sweet, delicate, calm, and warm canine is continually ready to please. From numerous points of view, the Cavalier makes an ideal house pet.

Supercilious King Charles Spaniels are upbeat as city or nation canines. Their delicate nature likewise makes them fantastic treatment canines. Their mouth contrasts from the King Charles Spaniel: the Cavalier gives off an impression of being grinning, with its mouth turned up, while the King Charles' mouth turns down.The tolerably long and sleek layer of the Cavalier King Charles, which is generally found in strong ruby, dark and tan, parti-hues Blenheim (white and ruby) and tricolor (dark, tan, and white), might be marginally wavy. A trait of this variety is that its feet have long tufts of hair. A sweet and delicate articulation is additionally normal of the variety.

The Cavalier's reasonably boned and marginally long body makes it a superb and exquisite toy spaniel. It has the structure of a working spaniel yet is somewhat littler. The canine's step, then, is free and rich, with a decent drive and reach.

The Cavalier King Charles spaniel is the relative of a little toy spaniel portrayed in numerous sixteenth, seventeenth and eighteenth

Century works of art of northern Europe. This canine was initially reproduced to warm laps in drafty palaces and on crisp carriage rides. A remedy written in Olde English for the Queen of England guides all her this "comforte canine" on her lap to treat a virus. The Cavalier's other activity was to pull in bugs and along these lines save their lords the bug communicated bubonic plague.

During Tudor occasions, toy spaniels were basic as women's pets and, under the Stuarts, they were given the illustrious title of

King Charles spaniel. Ruler Charles II was only here and there observed without a few Cavaliers at his heels, and he composed a pronouncement — still basically today — that his namesake spaniel be acknowledged in any open spot, including the Houses of Parliament, which were commonly beyond reach to creatures.

CHAPTER ONE

ITS APPEARANCE AND SIZE

Its minor figure is 12 to 13 inches high at the shrivels and 13 to 18 pounds (6 to 8 kilograms). It is among the biggest toy breeds. The substance of the Cavalier is particular for its sweet, delicate articulation that owes a lot to its enormous, round, dull earthy colored eyes, separate well. The skull is somewhat adjusted, and the gag full, yet somewhat tightened. The since quite a while ago, feathered ears, which are set high and wide on the crown, fan forward somewhat to outline the face when the canine is ready.

The neck is genuinely long and set on slanting shoulders. The chest is tolerably profound and the body is conservative. The tail is conveyed merrily when moving.

The coat is long, smooth and delicate and comes in four shading blends: red and white with a fractional red cover and ears and red patches on a white body; tricolor (highly contrasting with tan focuses); ruby (strong red); and dark and tan.

CHAPTER 2

ITS CARE

The Cavalier isn't appropriate for outside living. Its long coat requires brushing on interchange days. The canine requires a decent measure of activity normally, as a cavort in a safe region or a moderate on-chain walk.

The Cavalier King Charles spaniel is anything but difficult to keep. Ideal as a family canine or as an ally for "void nesters," the Cavalier loves to nestle and has been portrayed as the ideal lap canine. Despite the fact that these canines have a proclivity for loud welcome, Cavaliers for the most part are not defensive. Ordinary preparing is vital to keeping the Cavalier's jacket glossy. Minimal in excess of an exhaustive week after week brushing is required, notwithstanding routine washing and expert managing as wanted. Light shedding, which happens in the spring and fall, for the most part excites little notification.

Unceremonious King Charles Spaniel can live cheerfully pretty much anyplace. They do require day by day strolls and appreciate climbing, running on the sea shore and canine games, for example, nimbleness, flyball and rally. Be that as it may, they ought to be assumed into a cool position in extremely warm conditions. These exquisite brave canines need to kindly so they are commonly a breeze to prepare. They hold data for quite a while once they've learned and know precisely what's up. Arrogant King Charles Spaniel lives on normal nine to fourteen years and is inclined to microvalve coronary illness, the main source of death in the Cavalier King Charles Spaniel. The Cavalier is in any event multiple times bound to get this ailment than some other variety. You have to ensure that the mother and father didn't have any heart issue.

The Cavalier requires ordinary prepping and extraordinary consideration ought to be paid to the ears. They are inclined to tangling and tangling. You would need to ensure that they are slick and clean, on the grounds that with such a lovely canine, who might need to take a gander at a filthy Cavalier King Charles Spaniel?

The Cavalier King Charles Spaniel is a toy breed that develops to a normal of 13 to 18 pounds and they are very inviting and individuals situated. These canines have a life expectancy somewhere in the range of 10 and 14 years which is about normal for a canine of their size, perhaps a little on the low end. To guarantee that your Cavalier King Charles Spaniel carries on with a long and sound life, ensure you feed him a top notch diet produced using characteristic fixings and detailed to meet his high vitality prerequisites.

The Cavalier King Charles Spaniel is a functioning and lively variety who will tail you wherever you go. Like all canines, they need an equalization of protein and fat in their eating regimen to fabricate and keep up fit muscles and to give vitality to fuel their quick digestion systems. Both of these supplements should originate from excellent creature sources to guarantee bioavailability of the supplements. Meat, poultry, and fish are extraordinary wellsprings of complete protein for your canine and things like chicken fat and salmon oil give solid fats.

Despite the fact that the Cavalier King Charles Spaniel doesn't have explicit requirements for starches in his eating routine, these nourishments give dietary fiber just as fundamental supplements. Entire grains, bland vegetables, beans, and vegetables are probably the most absorbable types of sugars for canines. Notwithstanding protein, fat, and sugars, your canine additionally needs certain nutrients and minerals which originate from engineered supplements just as new leafy foods.

Pup Cavalier King Charles Spaniel Diet – As a little dog, your Cavalier King Charles Spaniel needs a high-vitality diet that gives at least 22% protein and 8% fat. Search for a little variety doggy formula to guarantee that this proportion is met.

Grown-up Cavalier King Charles Spaniel Diet – When your Cavalier King Charles Spaniel grows up, he'll need at least 18% protein and 5% fat in his eating routine, in a perfect world from excellent creature sources. A little variety grown-up formula is a decent method to ensure these requirements are met.

Senior Cavalier King Charles Spaniel Diet – When your Cavalier King Charles Spaniel turns into a senior around 7 to 9 years old, you may need to change him to a senior formula if his digestion eases back down. Heftiness is consistently hazardous yet especially so for senior canines.

With regards to an excellent eating routine for Cavalier King Charles Spaniels, you ought to likewise search for valuable enhancements. Chelated minerals have been artificially bound to protein particles which makes them all the more naturally important to your canine. Prebiotic filaments uphold sound gut verdure and probiotics uphold solid assimilation.

As a little variety canine, your Cavalier King Charles Spaniel has an extremely quick digestion. Most canines of this size require a normal of 30 to 40 calories for every pound of body weight every day. For most canine nourishments, this compares to about ½ to 1 cup of food for each day separated into a few dinners. Remember that the calorie substance of each canine food is extraordinary, so you'll have to allude to the taking care of proposals on the bundle as indicated by your canine's age, weight, and action level.

At the point when your Cavalier King Charles Spaniel is a little dog, he needs a consistent deluge of vitality. Most doggies excel on four little dinners daily. As your canine arrives at his grown-up size, you can change to three dinners every day and change to a little variety grown-up formula at a year. From that point, check your canine's weight at regular intervals and make changes in accordance with his eating regimen varying. Around 7 to 9 years, think about changing to a little variety senior formula or basically lessen the size of your canine's suppers.

CHAPTER 4

COMMON HEALTH PROBLEMS

The Cavalier King Charles Spaniel breed, which has a normal life expectancy of 9 to 14 years, may experience the ill effects of minor medical issues, for example, patellar luxation, and entropion, or serious issues like syringomelia, mitral valve infection (MVD), and canine hip dysplasia (CHD). Some of the time retinal dysplasia is found in the variety. Numerous Cavaliers additionally have diminished platelet numbers, however this doesn't appear to bring about any issues. Heart, eye, hip, and knee tests are recommended for this type of canine.

Here is a speedy rundown of the medical issues to which the Cavalier King Charles Spaniel might be inclined:

Hypersensitivities

Waterfalls

Ear Infections

Hip Dysplasia

Keratoconjucnctivitis

Mitral Valve Disease

Patellar Luxation

Essential Secretory Otitis Media

Skin Problems

Syringomyelia

CHAPTER 5

ITS COST

The normal expense of a Cavalier King Charles Spaniel canine is in the scope of $1,000 to $3,500. Factors, for example, raiser and shading influences the value you'll in the end pay for this canine. There's likewise the month to month upkeep cost required, up to $250 for care, food, and preparing.

CHAPTER 6

PREPPING ONE

As referenced, they have a solitary coat, which implies they have less hide on their body in general. Along these lines, as a rule, they won't shed as much hide consistently or shed as much during the adjustment in season as their twofold covered partners.

You can anticipate a moderate measure of shedding consistently, which can be decreased by a legitimate prepping custom.

They are not the most elevated upkeep breed out there, yet they are inclined to matts and tangles given the length of hair they have. This is especially obvious around their ears where it is longer.

It is prescribed to brush them 2-3 times each week to keep them tie free and that is about it. Customary brushing will assist with keeping abundance shedding under control by eliminating lose hide and expanding the characteristic oil content in your canine's skin.

To the extent washing, you should downplay this as they are a perfect canine, and over washing can cause dry skin, which can improve the probability of overabundance shedding.

It is alright to cut this sort of coat, in spite of the fact that redundant up to a standard brushing routine is kept.

For ordinary brushing, a fiber/pin brush combo will work and for matts and tangles you might need to investigate getting a slicker brush. The key is to brush normally to evade matts in any case, yet they do occur every once in a while.

THE END

Made in the USA
Las Vegas, NV
14 August 2021

28169772R00017